7 ducks!

How many ducks could fit in a **bus**, without any flapping, quacking, or fuss?

How Many Ducks Could Fit in a Bus?

CREATIVE WAYS TO LOOK AT VOLUME

by Clara Cella

PEBBLE
a capstone imprint

Could baby **birds** fit in a cup this small? YES! Turn the page! Let's count them all!

Squeal!
Squeeeeeal!
Rub-a-dub-dub!
How many
piglets could
fit in a tub?

5 piglets!

Look at
this **donut**.
Try not to drool!
How many
donuts could fit
in a pool?

8 donuts!

This square **box**
has lots to hide.
How many turtles
fit inside?

FRESH H

4 turtles!

OT PIZZA

Next comes
a sweet,
count-along treat:
a spoonful of
sugar **bees**
you can eat!

How many **fish** could fit in here, swimming in water cool and clear?

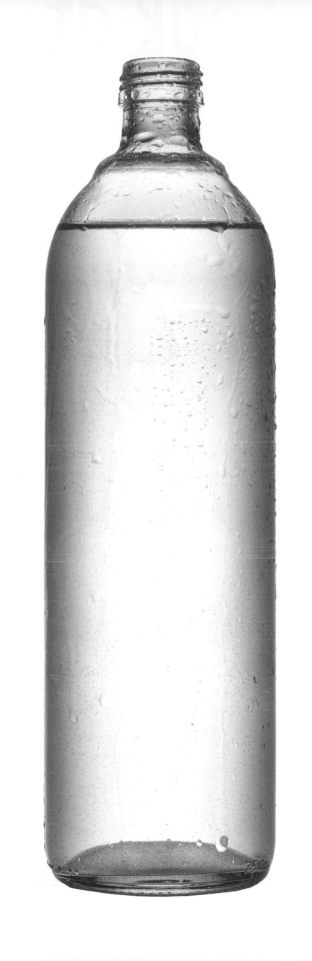

How many **friends** are sharing your lunch?

The basket is full, so I'd say A BUNCH!

LOOK FOR OTHER BOOKS IN THE SERIES:

How Many Flamingos Tall Is a Giraffe?

CREATIVE WAYS TO LOOK AT HEIGHT

by Clara Cella

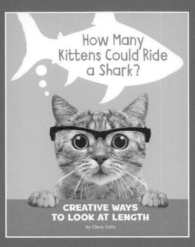

How Many Kittens Could Ride a Shark?

CREATIVE WAYS TO LOOK AT LENGTH

by Clara Cella

How Many Llamas Does a Car Weigh?

CREATIVE WAYS TO LOOK AT WEIGHT

by Clara Cella

Pebble Sprout is published by Pebble, an imprint of Capstone.
1710 Roe Crest Drive, North Mankato, Minnesota 56003
www.capstonepub.com

Library of Congress Cataloging-in-Publication Data
Names; Cella, Clara, author. Title; How many ducks could fit in a bus? ; creative ways to look at volume / by Clara Cella. Description; North Mankato, Minnesota ; Pebble, [2020] | Series; Silly measurements | Audience; Ages 4-6 | Audience; Grades K-1 | Summary; Eight outside-the-box measuring units, from ducks to donuts, introduce pre-readers to the math concept of volume. Wonderous composite photos and a dash of text illustrate the volume of a bus, a bathtub, a teacup, and more in fresh, non-standard ways;— Provided by publisher. Identifiers; LCCN 2019043653 (print) | LCCN 2019043654 (ebook) | ISBN 9781977113245 (hardcover) | ISBN 9781977120113 (paperback) | ISBN 9781977113283 (pdf) Subjects; LCSH; Volume (Cubic content)—Juvenile literature. | Measurement—Juvenile literature. Classification; LCC QC104 .C45 2020 (print) | LCC QC104 (ebook) | DDC 530.8—dc23 LC record available at https://lccn.loc.gov/2019043653 LC ebook record available at https//lccn.loc.gov/2019043654

Summary: Eight outside-the-box measuring units, from ducks to donuts, introduce pre-readers to the math concept of volume. Wonderous composite photos and a dash of text illustrate the volume of a bus, a bathtub, a teacup, and more in fresh, non-standard ways.

Image Credits
Capstone Studio: Karon Dubke, 23, 24, 25; Shutterstock: Africa Studio, 4–5 (room), Alison Henley, 7, 8–9, Andrey Armyagov, 28–29 (fish), Anton Starikov, 24–25 (spoon), Autobahn, 15, 16, 17, ben bryant, 12–13 (bathtub), dibrova, 5 (middle right), ESB Professional, cover (bus), back cover, Flashon Studio, 3, 4–5, Gerald A. DeBoer, 20 (turtles), 21 (bottom), grynold, 16–17 (pool), limpido, 27, 28–29, LittlePerfectStock, 11, 13 (top middle), Michiel de Wit, 21 (top), Sergei Kardashev, 20–21 (box), Sloth Astronaut, 19 (pizza slice logo), spawn101, cover (flower), 1, Tsekhmister, 5 (middle left), 12 (top middle), Viktar Savanevich, 8–9 (baby birds), vincent noel, 19, 20–21 (pizza logo), yevgeniy11, cover (duckling), 1, 4 (middle right), 12 (bottom middle), 13 (bottom middle), Yuliia Sonsedska, 4 (middle left), 13 (bottom right), 31 (raccoons), Yuri Samsonov, 30, 31

Editorial Credits
Editor: Jill Kalz; Designer: Ted Williams; Media Researcher: Svetlana Zhurkin; Production Specialist: Katy LaVigne